SATURN

The Ringed Wonder

by Ellen Lawrence

Consultants:

Suzy Gazlay, MA
Recipient, Presidential Award for Excellence in Science Teaching

Kevin Yates
Fellow of the Royal Astronomical Society

Published in 2014 by Ruby Tuesday Books Ltd.

Editor: Mark J. Sachner
Designer: Emma Randall

Photo Credits:
Ron Miller: 4–5. NASA: Cover, 6, 8, 10–11, 12–13, 14–15, 16–17, 18–19, 20–21. Ruby Tuesday Books: 7, 22. Shutterstock: 9.

Library of Congress Control Number: 2013939986

ISBN 978-1-909673-14-4

Printed and published in the United States of America

For further information including rights and permissions requests, please contact our Customer Service Department at 877-337-8577

Contents

Words shown in **bold** in the text are explained in the glossary.

Welcome to Saturn

Imagine flying to a world that is nearly a billion miles from Earth.

As your spacecraft gets close, you see this world is surrounded by huge rings.

The rings are made of dust and chunks of ice.

You manage to fly through the icy rings, but there is nowhere to land.

That's because this distant world is a gigantic ball of **gases** and liquids.

Welcome to the **planet** Saturn!

No humans have ever visited Saturn, but spacecraft have. The spacecraft sent information about the planet back to scientists on Earth.

This picture was created on a computer. It shows what it might look like to fly into the rings that circle around Saturn.

The Solar System

Saturn is moving through space at about 21,500 miles per hour (35,000 km/h).

It is moving around the Sun in a huge circle.

Saturn is one of eight planets circling the Sun.

The planets are called Mercury, Venus, our home planet Earth, Mars, Jupiter, Saturn, Uranus, and Neptune.

Icy **comets** and large rocks, called **asteroids**, are also moving around the Sun.

Together, the Sun, the planets, and other space objects are called the **solar system**.

Most of the asteroids in the solar system are in a ring called the asteroid belt.

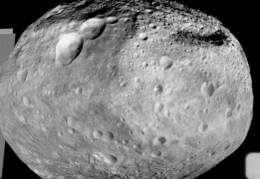

An asteroid

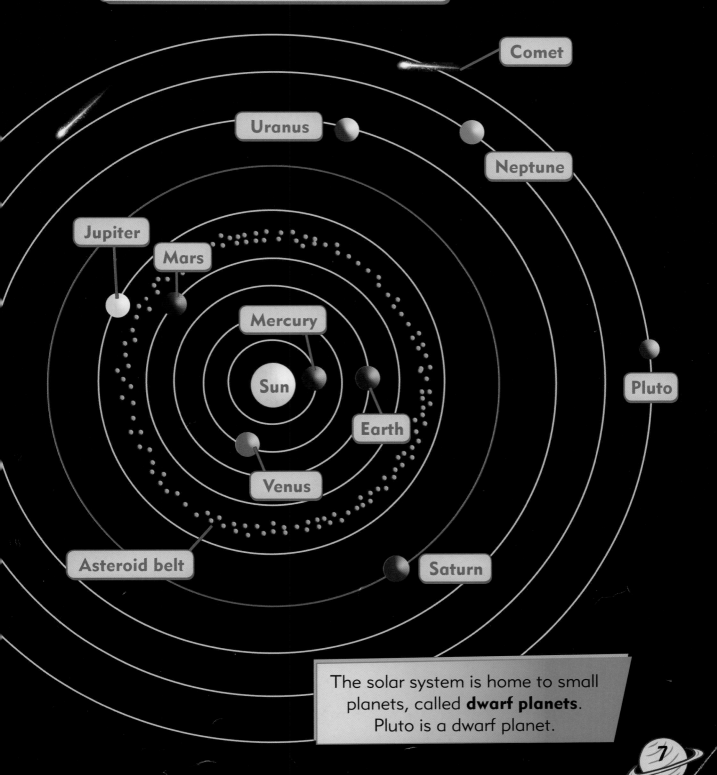

The Solar System
Saturn is the sixth planet from the Sun.

Comet

Uranus

Neptune

Jupiter

Mars

Mercury

Sun

Earth

Pluto

Venus

Asteroid belt

Saturn

The solar system is home to small planets, called **dwarf planets**.
Pluto is a dwarf planet.

Saturn's Amazing Journey

The time it takes a planet to **orbit**, or circle, the Sun once is called its year.

Earth takes just over 365 days to orbit the Sun, so a year on Earth lasts 365 days.

Saturn is farther from the Sun than Earth, so it must make a much longer journey.

It takes Saturn nearly 30 Earth years to orbit the Sun.

This means that a 30-year-old adult on Earth would just be turning 1 in Saturn years!

As a planet orbits the Sun, it also spins, or **rotates**, like a top.

Saturn

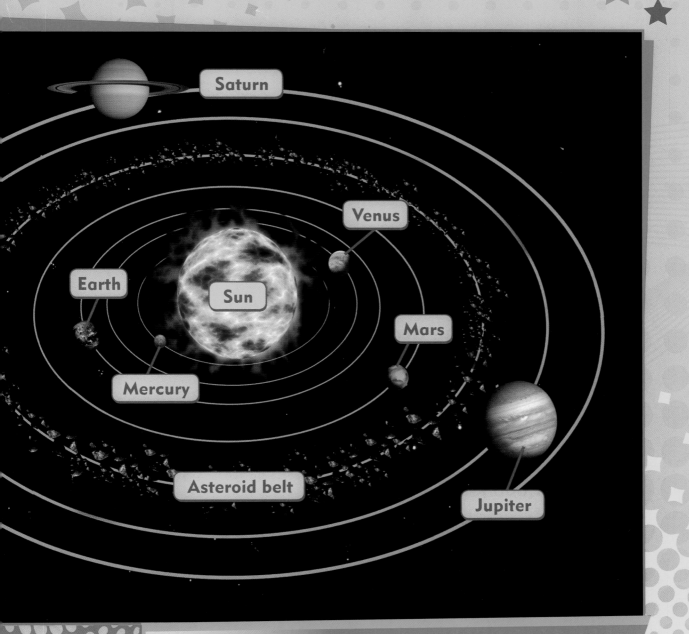

To orbit the Sun once, Earth makes a journey of nearly 584 million miles (940 million km). Saturn makes a much longer journey of about 5.5 billion miles (9 billion km).

A Closer Look at Saturn

Saturn is the second-largest planet in the solar system.

Unlike Earth, which is a rocky planet, Saturn doesn't have a solid surface.

The planet is surrounded by a thick layer of gases called an **atmosphere**.

Beneath its atmosphere, the planet is a gigantic ball of liquids.

Inside Saturn's atmosphere, super-fast winds blow at up to 1,000 miles per hour (1,600 km/h).

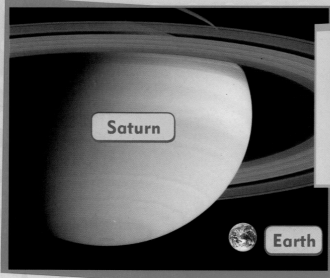

Saturn

Earth

In this picture, Earth and Saturn have been placed next to each other. The picture shows how huge Saturn is compared to Earth.

This photo shows a giant **hurricane** at Saturn's north pole. It was taken by a spacecraft named *Cassini* (kuh-SEE-nee) in April 2013. The red part is the eye, or center, of the hurricane.

Eye of hurricane

Close-up of eye of hurricane

This is a close-up of the eye of the hurricane on Saturn. The eye is 1,250 miles (2,000 km) across!

Saturn's Fantastic Rings

When you look at Saturn through a telescope, its rings look like solid, colorful circles.

They are actually made of billions of pieces of ice and dust.

The rings may have formed from pieces of **moons** and comets that came close to Saturn.

As these objects orbited the planet, they smashed into one another.

This created lots of chunks of ice and dust.

Over millions and billions of years, this icy rubble gathered together to form the rings.

Some of the pieces of ice and dust in Saturn's rings are as small as grains of sand. Others are as big as houses, while a few are the size of mountains!

Rings

Saturn

13

Saturn's Family of Moons

Saturn has a big family of small worlds circling around it.

These icy space objects are the huge planet's moons.

Earth, our home planet, has just one moon.

Saturn has at least 53 moons, and scientists think there may be more!

Saturn's biggest moon, Titan, is the second-largest moon in the solar system.

It is also the only moon in the solar system with an atmosphere.

Titan is much bigger than Earth's moon.

Earth's moon

Titan

Earth

Meet Some Moons!

The Splat

Rhea (REE-uh)

Many of Saturn's moons have holes called craters on their surfaces. The craters were made by space objects hitting the moons. Saturn's moon Rhea has a crater known as "The Splat!"

Epimetheus
(eh-pih-MEE-thee-us)

Mimas
(MI-muhs)

Hyperion
(hi-PEER-ee-uhn)

Enceladus
(en-SEL-eh-duhs)

Phoebe
(FEE-bee)

Iapetus
(i-AP-eh-tuhs)

A Mission to Saturn and Titan

In October 1997, a spacecraft named *Cassini* blasted off from Earth on a mission to study Saturn.

It reached Saturn in July 2004.

Cassini sent a small space **probe**, called *Huygens* (HOY-guhnz), to study Saturn's moon Titan.

As *Huygens* traveled through Titan's atmosphere, it took pictures and collected **data**.

It also collected information when it landed on the moon.

Huygens beamed the data it gathered back to *Cassini*.

Cassini

This photo shows scientists working on *Cassini*.

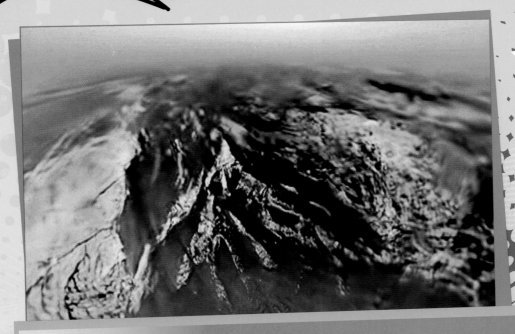

Huygens allowed scientists to see what was under Titan's atmosphere. It took this photo of mountains when it was about 5 miles (8 km) above Titan's surface.

Huygens probe

This step-by-step picture shows how Huygens might have looked as it landed on Titan. The probe was about the size of a car.

The Mission Goes On!

Cassini is still orbiting Saturn today.

As it flies around the planet, the spacecraft studies Saturn's rings and moons.

Every day, the spacecraft sends data back to scientists on Earth!

Cassini's mission should last until 2017, which will be 20 years since it left Earth.

Then, *Cassini*'s fantastic story will end when the spacecraft crashes itself into the planet below!

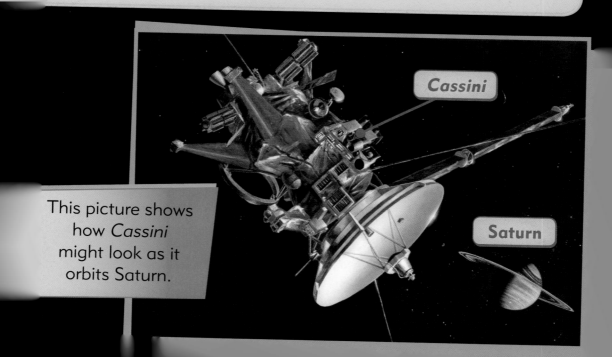

This picture shows how *Cassini* might look as it orbits Saturn.

Cassini

Saturn

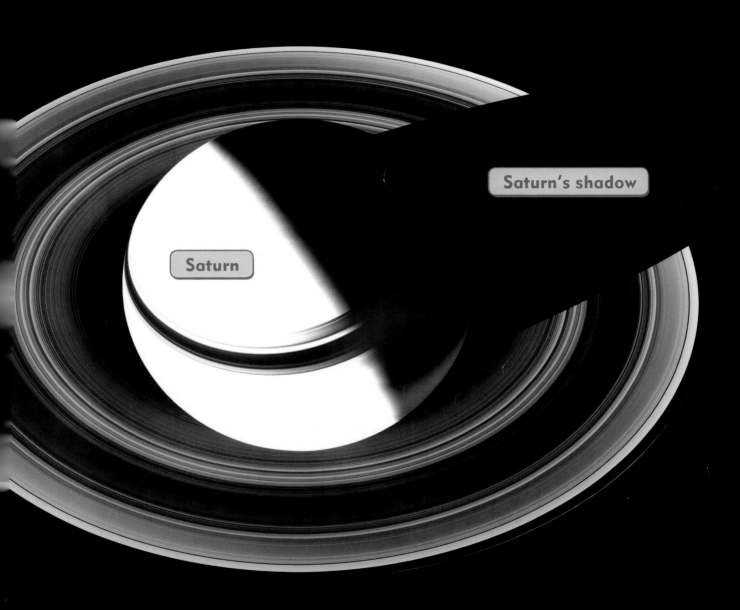

Saturn

Saturn's shadow

This photo was taken by *Cassini*. It shows Saturn facing the Sun. The planet's huge shadow can be seen behind it.

Saturn Fact File

Here are some key facts about Saturn, the sixth planet from the Sun.

Discovery of Saturn

Saturn can be seen in the sky without a telescope. People have known it was there since ancient times.

How Saturn got its name

The planet is named after the Roman god of farming.

Planet sizes

This picture shows the sizes of the solar system's planets compared to each other.

Sun
Mercury
Earth
Venus
Mars
Jupiter
Saturn
Uranus
Neptune

Saturn's size

About 72,367 miles (116,464 km) across

How long it takes for Saturn to rotate once

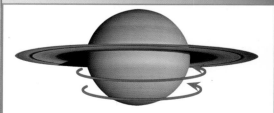

About 10.5 Earth hours

Saturn's distance from the Sun

The closest Saturn gets to the Sun is 838,741,509 miles (1,349,823,615 km).

The farthest Saturn gets from the Sun is 934,237,322 miles (1,503,509,229 km).

Length of Saturn's orbit around the Sun

5,565,935,315 miles (8,957,504,604 km)

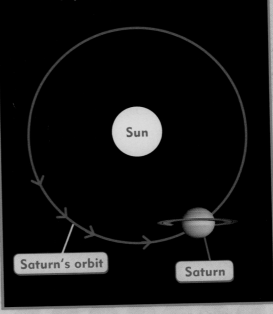

Sun

Saturn's orbit

Saturn

Average speed at which Saturn orbits the Sun

21,562 miles per hour (34,701 km/h)

Length of a year on Saturn

Nearly 11,000 Earth days (nearly 30 Earth years)

Saturn's Moons

Saturn has at least 53 moons. There are possibly more to be discovered.

Temperature on Saturn

-288°F (-178°C)

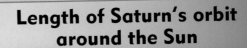

Get Crafty
Sparkly Saturn

When the Sun's light reflects, or bounces, off Saturn's rings, it makes the chunks of ice sparkle. Make your own sparkly Saturn using paint and glitter.

You will need:

- Construction paper
- A saucer
- A pencil
- Scissors
- Paint and a paintbrush
- White glue
- Glitter
- A ruler

1. To make Saturn, place a saucer upside down on the paper and draw around it. Cut out the circle.

2. To make Saturn's rings, draw an oval shape that is twice as wide as the circle, and cut it out.

Oval   Circle

3. Paint the circle. What colors will you use to show Saturn's clouds and gases?

4. Cover the oval shape with glue. Sprinkle glitter over the oval shape, until all the glue is covered. When the glue is dry, carefully tip any loose glitter back into the glitter container.

5. Measure the width of Saturn, then ask an adult to help you cut a slot the length of Saturn's width in the oval shape.

Slot

6. Finally, slide Saturn into the slot so it is surrounded by its glittery rings.

asteroid (AS-teh-royd) A large rock that is orbiting the Sun. An asteroid can be as small as a car or bigger than a mountain.

atmosphere (AT-muh-sfeer) A layer of gases around a planet, moon, or star.

comet (KAH-mit) A space object made of ice, rock, and dust that is orbiting the Sun.

data (DAY-tuh) Facts and other types of information that are gathered and studied.

dwarf planet (DWARF PLAN-et) A round object in space that is orbiting the Sun. Dwarf planets are much smaller than the eight main planets.

gas (GASS) A substance, such as oxygen or helium, that does not have a definite shape or size.

hurricane (HUR-uh-kane) A huge storm with powerful winds that circle around the center, or eye, of the storm. A hurricane can be hundreds of miles wide, and the winds can reach speeds of 200 miles per hour (320 km/h).

moon (MOON) An object in space that is orbiting a planet. Moons are usually made of rock, or rock and ice. Some are just a few miles wide. Others are hundreds of miles wide.

orbit (OR-bit) To circle, or move around, another object.

planet (PLAN-et) A large object in space that is orbiting the Sun. Some planets, such as Saturn, are made of gases and liquids. Others, such as Earth, are made of rock.

probe (PROBE) A spacecraft that does not have any people aboard. Probes are usually sent to planets or other objects in space to take photographs and collect information. They are controlled by scientists on Earth.

rotate (ROH-tate) To spin around.

solar system (SOH-ler SIS-tem) The Sun and all the objects that orbit it, such as planets, their moons, asteroids, and comets.

Index

Read More

Allyn, Daisy. *Saturn: The Ringed Planet (Our Solar System).* New York: Gareth Stevens (2011).

Hughes, Catherine D. *First Big Book of Space (National Geographic Little Kids).* Washington, D.C.: The National Geographic Society (2012).

Learn More Online

To learn more about Saturn, go to
www.rubytuesdaybooks.com/saturn